STRATEGIES
FOR TEACHING
Middle-Level and
High School Keyboard

MENC wishes to thank
Carolynn A. Lindeman for developing and coordinating this series;
Martha F. Hilley and *Tommie Pardue*
for selecting, writing, and editing the strategies for this book;
and the following teachers for submitting strategies:

Lynn Andreas

Stephan P. Barnicle

Anna Belle Bognar

Janice Judy Buckner

Carla Carroll

Ann Cissell

Carolyn Garner

Pat Graham

Dianne Hardy

Marianne Holland

Louise Jackson

Bobbie B. Jones

Ginna Kelley

Julia Kohring

Rachel Kramer

Colleen Tosi Ludeker

Claudia McCain

Mary J. Nelson

Lynn E. Purse

Veronica Shaver

Michael Skinner

Joanne Spivey

Fred Wein

YOUR KEY TO
IMPLEMENTING
THE NATIONAL
STANDARDS
FOR MUSIC
EDUCATION

STRATEGIES
FOR TEACHING

Middle-Level and
High School Keyboard

COMPILED
AND EDITED
BY
Martha F. Hilley

and

Tommie Pardue

MENC
MENC
MENC
MENC

MUSIC EDUCATORS NATIONAL CONFERENCE

CONTENTS

PREFACE. vii

INTRODUCTION. 1

STRATEGIES FOR GRADES 5–8. 3

Standard 1
Singing, alone and with others, a varied
repertoire of music 5

Standard 2
Performing on instruments, alone and
with others, a varied repertoire of music 7

Standard 3
Improvising melodies, variations, and
accompaniments. 13

Standard 4
Composing and arranging music within
specified guidelines. 17

Standard 5
Reading and notating music 21

Standard 6
Listening to, analyzing, and describing
music 27

Standard 7
Evaluating music and music
performances 28

Standard 8
Understanding relationships between
music, the other arts, and disciplines
outside the arts. 31

Standard 9
Understanding music in relation to history
and culture 32

STRATEGIES FOR GRADES 9–12 . . . . **35**

Standard 1
Singing, alone and with others, a varied
repertoire of music **37**

Standard 2
Performing on instruments, alone and
with others, a varied repertoire of music **38**

Standard 3
Improvising melodies, variations, and
accompaniments. **44**

Standard 4
Composing and arranging music within
specified guidelines **48**

Standard 5
Reading and notating music **51**

Standard 6
Listening to, analyzing, and describing
music **53**

Standard 7
Evaluating music and music
performances **55**

Standard 8
Understanding relationships between
music, the other arts, and disciplines
outside the arts. **56**

Standard 9
Understanding music in relation to history
and culture **57**

RESOURCES **59**

PREFACE

The Music Educators National Conference (MENC) created the
Strategies for Teaching series to help preservice and in-service music
educators implement the K–12 National Standards for Music
Education and the MENC Prekindergarten Standards. To address the
many components of the school music curriculum, each book in the
series focuses on a specific curricular area and a particular level. The
result is eleven books spanning the K–12 areas of band, chorus, general music, strings/orchestra, guitar, keyboard, and specialized ensembles. A prekindergarten book and a guide for college music methods
classes complete the series.

The purpose of the series is to seize the opportunity presented by the
landmark education legislation of 1994. With the passage of the
Goals 2000: Educate America Act, the arts were established for the
first time in our country's history as a core, challenging subject in
which all students need to demonstrate competence. Voluntary acad-
emic standards were called for in all nine of the identified core subjects—standards specifying what students need to know and be able
to do when they exit grades 4, 8, and 12.

In music, content and achievement standards were drafted by an
MENC task force. They were examined and commented on by music
teachers across the country, and the task force reviewed their comments and refined the standards. While all students in grades K–8 are
expected to meet the achievement standards specified for those levels,
two levels of achievement—proficient and advanced—are designated
for students in grades 9–12. Students who elect music courses for one
to two years beyond grade 8 are expected to perform at the proficient
level. Students who elect music courses for three to four years beyond
grade 8 are expected to perform at the advanced level.

The music standards, together with the dance, theatre, and visual arts
standards, were presented in final form—*National Standards for Arts
Education*—to the U.S. Secretary of Education in March 1994.
Recognizing the importance of early childhood education, MENC
went beyond the K–12 standards and established content and
achievement standards for the prekindergarten level as well, which are
included in MENC's *The School Music Program: A New Vision*.

Now the challenge at hand is to implement the standards at the state
and local levels. Implementation may require schools to expand the

resources necessary to achieve the standards as specified in MENC's *Opportunity-to-Learn Standards for Music Instruction: Grades PreK–12.* Teachers will need to examine their curricula to determine if they lead to achievement of the standards. For many, the standards reflect exactly what has always been included in the school music curriculum—they represent best practice. For others, the standards may call for some curricular expansion.

To assist in the implementation process, this series offers teaching strategies illustrating how the music standards can be put into action in the music classroom. The strategies themselves do not suggest a curriculum. That, of course, is the responsibility of school districts and individual teachers. The strategies, however, are designed to help in curriculum development, lesson planning, and assessment of music learning.

The teaching strategies are based on the content and achievement standards specified in the *National Standards for Arts Education* (K–12) and *The School Music Program: A New Vision* (PreK–12). Although the strategies, like the standards, are designed primarily for four-year-olds, fourth graders, eighth graders, and high school seniors, many may be developmentally appropriate for students in other grades. Each strategy, a lesson appropriate for a portion of a class session or a complete class session, includes an objective (a clear statement of what the student will be able to do), a list of necessary materials, a description of what prior student learning and experiences are expected, a set of procedures, and the indicators of success. A follow-up section identifies ways learning may be expanded.

The *Guide for Music Methods Classes* contains strategies appropriate for preservice instructional settings in choral, instrumental, and general music methods classes. The teaching strategies in this guide relate to the other books in the series and reflect a variety of teaching/learning styles.

Bringing a series of thirteen books from vision to reality in a little over a year's time required tremendous commitment from many, many music educators—not to mention the tireless help of the MENC publications staff. Literally hundreds of music teachers across the country answered the call to participate in this project, the largest such participation in an MENC publishing endeavor. The contributions of these teachers and the books' editors are proudly presented in the various publications.

—*Carolynn A. Lindeman*
Series Editor

Carolynn A. Lindeman, professor of music at San Francisco State University, served on the MENC task force that developed the music education standards. She is the author of three college textbooks (The Musical Classroom, PianoLab, *and* MusicLab) *and numerous articles.*

INTRODUCTION

This publication provides suggested keyboard activities to be used for implementation of the standards within the middle grades and high school. Some of the suggested teaching strategies call for equipment usually found in general music classrooms; other strategies are designed for technology-specific group piano classrooms. It is not the intent to suggest that all schools have full-blown keyboard programs complete with electronic keyboards. For many, this may be a goal. Educators have discovered that many students have keyboards at home and are often more than willing to bring these instruments to school. This has solved problems with equipment shortages in many learning situations and allowed students to share their keyboards with peers.

The time allocated for music instruction during the regular school day will determine the level of proficiency that students are able to achieve. Scheduling of general music classes varies from once weekly to as much as one hour daily for the school year. Classes devoted specifically to instruction in piano frequently are scheduled on a daily basis for the entire school year.

The teaching strategies presented here address both general music and keyboard programs. Most are written to give the keyboard the role of facilitator of music education, a means of reinforcing concepts and providing skills assessment. Most may stand on their own or serve as possible springboards for further creative ideas.

Under the Materials heading for each strategy, keyboards are generally not listed because either acoustic or electronic instruments may be used. If electronic keyboards or some other technology is required, the instruments or equipment is listed under the Materials heading for that strategy. Similarly, if an acoustic keyboard is required, pianos are listed under that heading.

There are several steps listed under the Procedures section of each strategy. While these steps follow sequentially, they should be considered as suggestions that will help the students to experience success in readily meeting the objectives. In some cases, it may not be necessary to include every step found in the Procedures section. The teacher should make this determination. The use of tutorial software programs to help students reinforce such skills as pitch and rhythm accuracy is another possible follow-up step for certain strategies.

This book is not intended to serve as a complete guide for keyboard education. Each teacher must assess the needs of his or her own students and program and plan music instruction to meet those needs. The strategies in this book will, however, provide the teacher with instructional models for incorporating keyboards into a middle or high school music curriculum while helping students work toward meeting the National Standards for Music Education.

STRATEGIES
Grades 5–8

STANDARD 1B

Singing, alone and with others, a varied repertoire of music: Students sing with expression and technical accuracy a repertoire of vocal literature with a level of difficulty of 2, on a scale of 1 to 6, including some songs performed from memory.

Objective

- Students will sing and play a selection with appropriate expression and accurate pitches and rhythm.

Materials

- "Jamaica Farewell," in *The Music Connection,* Grade 6 (Parsippany, NJ: Silver Burdett Ginn, 1995), with accompanying CD; or *World of Music,* Grade 6 (Parsippany, NJ: Silver Burdett Ginn, 1991), with accompanying CD
- Teacher-generated chord tone chart
- CD player

Prior Knowledge and Experiences

- Students have formed and played tetrachord major scales.
- Students have had experience singing melodic lines with and without accompaniment.

Procedures

1. Ask students to follow the melody of "Jamaica Farewell" as you play the recording. Ask them to listen carefully to the phrasing of the melodic line and its relation to the text and the syncopation of the rhythm.

2. Have students sing the melodic line with appropriate expression along with the recording. Ask them to pay particular attention to accuracy of the syncopated rhythm and accuracy of pitch. Repeat until singing is secure.

3. Have students sing the melodic line as they tap on top of the keyboard one whole note for each measure of the song. Remind them that whole notes must occur on the downbeat at all times.

4. Display the chord tone chart:

   ‖: C   F   G   C :‖

   ‖: C   Dm   G   C :‖

5. On the keyboard, have students cover the C through G keys with their left hands. Then have them select the individual fingers that fall on the appropriate letter names (C = 5, D = 4, E = 3, F = 2, and G = 1) and play line 1 of the chord tone chart. Have them repeat the process with line 2.

6. Play the recording once again as students play whole notes on pitches of the chord tone chart. Repeat as students sing along with their chord tone accompaniment and the recording.

7. Ask students to accompany themselves, without the recording, as they sing "Jamaica Farewell."

Indicators of Success

- Students sing "Jamaica Farewell" and play a chord tone accompaniment with accurate pitches and rhythm and with appropriate expression.

(continued)

Follow-up

- Determine an appropriate rhythmic ostinato for the chord tone accompaniment and play it while some of the students play the countermelody (indicated in the text) on bells.
- Have all students sing as they accompany on their particular parts.

STANDARD 2A

Performing on instruments, alone and with others, a varied repertoire of music: Students perform on at least one instrument accurately and independently, alone and in small and large ensembles, with good posture, good playing position, and good breath, bow, or stick control.

Objective

- Demonstrating balance in parts, students will perform accurately an ensemble accompaniment to a given melody using a counter-melody (descant), chords, and bass line.

Materials

- "Streets of Laredo," in *The Music Connection,* Grade 5 (Parsippany, NJ: Silver Burdett Ginn, 1995), with Resource Book and accompanying CD
- CD player
- Electronic keyboards and headsets

Prior Knowledge and Experiences

- Students have formed and played tetrachord major scales. Using a printed model in the key of C major, they have discovered chords within the D, G, and A major tetra-chord scales.
- Students have studied sightreading at the keyboard from one-, two-, and five-line staves.

Procedures

1. Ask the students to follow the melody of the song "Streets of Laredo" as they listen to the recording. On a second listening, direct their attention to the descant.

2. Ask the students to notice when the descant is played and when the descant is sung. (It is played in verses 1 and 3 and sung in verses 2, 3, and 5.)

3. Direct the students to the performance score (p. 221 in the Resource Book). Have them determine logical fingerings for Part 1 of the ensemble accompaniment. (Hint: There are two positions—fourth finger on D and second finger on F-sharp.)

4. Play the recording again and have half the class sing and the other half play Part 1 of the ensemble accompaniment on verses 2, 3, and 5 when the descant is sung on the recording.

5. Allow at least two sets of students, using headsets, to practice all three parts of the ensemble accompaniment. (Part 1 is played only on verses 1 and 3.) Have the students practice the last four measures as an introduction for the singers.

6. Arrange a class performance: Ask for a minimum of six students to be keyboard players (two to each part of the ensemble accompaniment). Have other class members sing the song as written, with at least three individuals designated to sing the descant on verses 2, 3, and 5. Have students evaluate the performance by discussing ensemble balance, accuracy in parts, and so forth.

Indicators of Success

- Students give a successful ensemble performance of a musical arrangement that includes a countermelody, chords, and a bass line to a given melody.

Follow-up

- Ask students, with some playing from the song in their book, to turn the three-part ensemble accompaniment into a piano ensemble by adding the melody as part four.

STANDARD 2B

Performing on instruments, alone and with others, a varied repertoire of music: Students perform with expression and technical accuracy on at least one string, wind, percussion, or classroom instrument a repertoire of instrumental literature with a level of difficulty of 2, on a scale of 1 to 6.

Objective

- Through analysis, students will determine repetition, variation, and form in a keyboard selection (graded late elementary level) and perform accurately with careful attention to expression and phrasing.

Materials

- "Summer Mood," in *Pop! Goes the Piano,* Book 1 (Van Nuys, CA: Alfred Publishing Company, 1985)

Prior Knowledge and Experiences

- Students have studied harmonic and melodic intervals, major pentascales, root position triads, and sequential fingering.

Procedures

1. Have students listen while you play "Summer Mood." After they hear the music, ask students to look at the music (both the right-hand and the left-hand parts) and discover what "looks familiar." (Harmonic fifths)

2. Ask students to discuss the use of repetition. (Refer them to measures 1, 2, 3; 5, 6, 7; 25, 26, 27; and 29, 30, 31.) Ask them why measures 13, 14, and 15 and measures 37, 38, and 39 were excluded. (They are different.)

3. Ask students what is different in measures 9 to 12. (Movement is not stepwise; the movement goes up and down by skip.) Where do they see this again? (Measures 33 to 36) Have students discuss the relationship of the right hand in measure 4 to the right hand in measure 8.

4. Ask students to determine the form of "Summer Mood." (ABA codetta)

5. Discuss the importance of sequential fingering in the A and B sections.

6. Ask students what has changed in the first half of the codetta. (In measures 41 to 42, the mode changes to minor.)

7. Lead the students in a reading of "Summer Mood." Have students repeat the piece several times, paying careful attention to dynamics and phrasing.

Indicators of Success

- Students identify, aurally and visually, similar and different phrases and the musical form of the selection that they are performing.

Follow-up

- Ask students to play "Summer Mood" by memory at the next class meeting.

- Ask students to identify like and different phrases and musical forms in at least two other pieces of music.

STANDARD 2C

Performing on instruments, alone and with others, a varied repertoire of music:
Students perform music representing diverse genres and cultures, with
expression appropriate for the work being peformed.

Objective

■ Using contrasting ensemble versions that they have worked together to create for acoustic instruments (including the piano) and for electronic instruments (including the keyboard), students will perform with appropriate expression their arrangements of "We Shall Overcome."

Materials

■ "We Shall Overcome," music and several recordings from any reliable source, such as *The Music Connection,* Grade 8 (Parsippany, NJ: Silver Burdett Ginn, 1995)

■ Audio-playback equipment

■ Acoustic instruments, including the piano

■ Electronic instruments, including the keyboard

Prior Knowledge and Experiences

■ Students have listened to and discussed two different recordings of "We Shall Overcome," one performed with acoustic instruments and one performed with electronic instruments.

Procedures

1. Divide the students into groups and explain that one group will develop an acoustic ensemble performance and the other an electronic ensemble performance of "We Shall Overcome." Ask the students to make lists of ideas to be explored. These should include possibilities for each ensemble's performance. Explain that each student in the group must participate in at least one version of the two ensemble performances.

2. For the acoustic ensemble performance, have a group, for example, assign two members to play single lines on the piano (or a melody part and a chord part) and two or more members to be singers. Also ask them to add some appropriate percussion accompanying instruments and other elements that are available in the classroom.

3. For the electronic equipment version, have the students include synthesizer sounds, electronic keyboard ensemble parts that are the same as those played on the acoustic piano (or completely different parts), preset rhythm patterns or rhythm patterns developed by the students especially for this ensemble, and various appropriate preset special effect sounds or prerecorded sequencer tracks (depending on available equipment).

4. Allow the student groups time to experiment with their ideas, to reach decisions about what will be included in the two ensemble versions and how they will be handled, and to rehearse for the in-class performance. Depending on the amount of time, all of the song or just one phrase of the song can be used for this activity.

5. Have each student group perform for the class, first giving a brief verbal explanation of how the group reached decisions for its performance.

Indicators of Success

■ Through performance, students demonstrate the ability to express music of diverse genres and cultures in an instrumental ensemble experience of their own creation.

(continued)

- Students have a basic (though not extensive) background in music reading at the keyboard, chord skills, and electronic equipment operation skills.

Follow-up

- Ask students to collaborate to develop and perform ensembles using songs of other cultures (for example, Native American, Spanish, or Japanese songs).

STANDARD 2D

Performing on instruments, alone and with others, a varied repertoire of music:
Students play by ear simple melodies on a melodic instrument and
simple accompaniments on a harmonic instrument.

Objective

■ Students will play by ear a simple keyboard accompaniment to a familiar song.

Materials

■ Song sheets of several melodies (including "Poor Wayfaring Stranger") with indicated chord changes

■ Electronic keyboards and headsets

Prior Knowledge and Experiences

■ Students have sung the melody of "Poor Wayfaring Stranger" and have located individual notes of the keyboard accompaniment on their instruments.

■ Students have been introduced to triads.

Procedures

1. Ask the class to sing the melody of "Poor Wayfaring Stranger" as you demonstrate the accompaniment at the keyboard.

2. Have the students, by ear, play each chord used in the closest position (with each pitch of one chord moving to the "closest" pitch of the subsequent chord), right hand only.

3. Have the students, by ear, practice changing from chord to chord in tempo, right hand only.

4. Ask the students to suggest accompaniment styles to complement the song (block chords in steady rhythmic pulse; broken chords as single pitches; rhythmic variety).

5. Have the students, using headsets, practice the chosen accompaniment style.

6. Ask small groups or individuals to play the accompaniment while the class sings the melody.

7. Invite student accompanist(s) as well as other students to critique the performance.

Indicators of Success

■ Students accurately play by ear a keyboard accompaniment to a given song.

Follow-up

■ Lead a class discussion of the student performances, helping students to determine what they liked best about different student performances or what they would like to see changed about a particular performance.

■ Have students create a two-handed accompaniment by playing the root of each chord with the left hand while playing the triad with the right hand.

STANDARD 2E

Performing on instruments, alone and with others, a varied repertoire of music: Students perform with expression and technical accuracy a varied repertoire of instrumental literature with a level of difficulty of 3, on a scale of 1 to 6, including some solos performed from memory.

Objective

- Students will compare and contrast a variety of musical genres from a late elementary piano method book and perform them with expression and technical accuracy on the keyboard.

Materials

- "Festive March," "Waltz Pantomime," "Light and Blue," "Fandango," and "Scherzo," in *Piano Lesson Book,* Level 3, from *Alfred's Basic Piano Library* (Van Nuys, CA: Alfred Publishing Company, 1982)
- Chalkboard or chart (see step 2)

Prior Knowledge and Experiences

- Students have performed warm-up exercises that incorporate rhythm patterns, technique, and notation found in the selected pieces.
- Students have played ensemble arrangements of the selected pieces in piano class.

Procedures

1. Play the first eight measures of each piece on the keyboard. Ask students to categorize the music according to the nature of the piece (for example, march, waltz, blues, dance, classical).

2. Prepare a chart listing each piece of music with headings for meter signatures, key signature (major or minor), dynamic markings, note/rhythm patterns, chord structures, phrasing, and tempo. To complete the chart, ask the students to analyze each piece according to these headings.

3. Ask the students to compare the pieces for similarities as well as contrasts. Give specific examples (the use of triple meter for both the waltz and fandango songs, yet separate rhythm patterns for each). Ask volunteers to play through several measures of each piece on the keyboard to illustrate the point.

4. Have students play all musical selections in ensemble. Remind students to play with expression. Critique the technical performance in order to enhance the overall interpretation of the songs. Upon completion of each piece, ask students to continue to identify, compare, contrast, and analyze distinguishing characteristics.

5. Lead students in a discussion of expressive elements and their effect (for example, What kind of mood does each piece project? How do you feel when you play each piece?).

Indicators of Success

- Students identify various elements, such as rhythmic patterns, dynamics, chord structures, or melodic motifs, that distinguish categories or songs in a varied repertoire of music and perform the music with expression and technical accuracy.

Follow-up

- Ask students to find and perform additional examples of repertoire as categorized in the lesson (for example, "Calypso Rhumba," in *Ensemble Book,* Level 3, from *Alfred's Basic Piano Library).*

STANDARD 3A

Improvising melodies, variations, and accompaniments:
Students improvise simple harmonic accompaniments.

Objective

- Students will improvise a chordal (block- or broken-chord) accompaniment to a simple melody.

Materials

- "Festive March," in *Piano Lesson Book,* Level 3, from *Alfred's Basic Piano Library* (Van Nuys, CA: Alfred Publishing Company, 1982)

Prior Knowledge and Experiences

- Students can build block-chord patterns I, IV, and V7 in the keys of C, G, and D.

- Students have mastered the song "Festive March," as written.

Procedures

1. Have students identify the harmonic rhythm of "Festive March" (one chord per measure).

2. Have students name each chord in the song by scale step number (I, IV, or V7). Have students write the number name above each chord.

3. Have students play the chords in block style using their left hands.

4. Define and demonstrate broken-style chords. Have students experiment playing broken chords with their left hands. Then have them play broken chords using the harmonic rhythm of the piece.

5. With students working in pairs, have one student play the melody while the other one improvises, first using block-chord accompaniment and then using broken-chord accompaniment. Then ask them to switch parts.

Indicators of Success

- Students identify patterns of I, IV, and V7 chords in block form and improvise these patterns in a broken-chord style as an accompaniment to a simple melody.

Follow-up

- Encourage students to find other songs in the book and improvise broken chords in place of block chords. Demonstrate how the newly learned broken-chord format can be used in 4/4 meter by playing one note of the broken-chord pattern on each of the four beats of the measure.

- For students in Grades 7 and 8, demonstrate a rhythm of broken chords using two chord patterns per measure with a rhythm of eighth notes. The following pages in *Piano Lesson Book,* Level 3, are suggested: 10–11, 19, 22–23, and 28–29.

STANDARD 3B

Improvising melodies, variations, and accompaniments: *Students improvise melodic embellishments and simple rhythmic and melodic variations on given pentatonic melodies and melodies in major keys.*

Objective

- Students will identify familiar melodies as either major or pentatonic after playing them by ear and will improvise a rhythmic or melodic variation based on one of the melodies.

Materials

- Teacher-generated handouts listing titles of familiar songs, including some pentatonic and some major key songs (see step 3)
- Manuscript paper
- Electronic keyboards and headsets

Prior Knowledge and Experiences

- Students have played selected pentatonic and major scales on the keyboard or other classroom instruments.
- Students have played a few simple folk songs by ear and have experimented with rhythmic or melodic changes in learned keyboard examples.

Procedures

1. Have students review, write out, and play selected pentatonic and major scales.

2. Ask selected individual students to play their choice of one scale type or the other (the five-note major pentascale or the five-note pentatonic scale). Have the class identify aurally which type of scale was performed.

3. Distribute the handouts containing a short list of familiar song titles that are within the students' abilities to play by ear and are in either pentatonic or major. (This list might include "Amazing Grace" as an example for pentatonic or "Joy to the World" as an example for major. The first few notes of each melody can be printed next to the title if students need this help to get a good start on the activity.)

4. Ask students, using keyboard headsets and working individually or two to a keyboard, to play the melodies and write either "pentatonic" or "major" next to each song title. Discuss the answers with the students.

5. Have each student (or pair of students) choose one of the songs and improvise a variation based on either changing the rhythm or changing the melody.

6. Have students perform their variations for the class. Students listening to performances should see how many songs they can recognize even though rhythmic or melodic changes have been made.

Indicators of Success

- Students perform their song variations and accurately identify the scales of the songs as either pentatonic or major.

Follow-up

- Have students identify simple pentatonic or major melodies from printed notation. Have them create rhythmic or melodic improvisations based on these melodies.

STANDARD 3C

Improvising melodies, variations, and accompaniments: Students improvise short melodies, unaccompanied and over given rhythmic accompaniments, each in a consistent style, meter, and tonality.

Objective

- Using a given abbreviated blues scale and two given scat rhythms, students will improvise blues melodies.

Materials

- 12-bar blues form written on the chalkboard or on a hand-out
- Keyboard sheets with full-sized keys

Prior Knowledge and Experiences

- Students have studied the origins of the blues (call and response), have listened to some recordings of blues singers (for example, Ella Fitzgerald, Mel Tormé, and Cab Calloway), and have sung some blues on scat syllables in a predetermined context.
- Students have been introduced to the 12-bar blues form.
- Students know how to find C on the keyboard.

Procedures

1. Review the 12-bar blues form, referring to the chalkboard or the handout, and play an example of melodic improvisation using only the following two scat rhythms:

   Rhythm 1 (musical notation)

   Rhythm 2 (musical notation)

2. Have students review and practice an abbreviated blues scale (five-note scale: C, E-flat, F, G-flat, G).

3. Have students learn the first scat rhythm by verbalizing, tapping, and then playing on keyboard sheets. Have them use a simple pattern (for example, the quarter note on C and the eighth note on E-flat).

4. Ask students to listen while you play through the 12-bar blues, using the first scat rhythm and the notes C and E-flat in each measure in the right hand and playing a blues progression (with open fifths) in the left hand. Then, as you play the blues progression several times, have all students play the first scat rhythm together, using the notes C and E-flat. (This step will give students the opportunity to produce a given scat pattern successfully in context; that is, while listening to a 12-bar blues progression.)

5. Repeat steps 3 and 4 with the second scat rhythm. For this rhythm, have the students use a pattern similar to the first (for example, alternating the notes C and E-flat, with an accent on the last E-flat).

6. Have students use the first scat rhythm and improvise new melodies using the abbreviated blues scale from step 2. Have them do the same using the second scat rhythm.

7. Ask individual students to demonstrate independence in changing between the two scat rhythms. Then ask individual students to play four-bar phrases ("trading fours"—alternating among students until all have played a four-bar phrase).

(continued)

Indicators of Success

- Students improvise melodies using the given abbreviated blues scale and scat rhythms.

- Students make decisions about changing between the two scat rhythms within the 12-bar form.

Follow-up

- Add an advanced sequencer accompaniment to enhance the performance.

- Have students improvise harmonic "comping" patterns (patterns of regularly and/or irregularly spaced chords that punctuate and complement the melody), using scat syllables as rhythmic impetus.

STANDARD 4A

Composing and arranging music within specified guidelines: Students compose short pieces within specified guidelines, demonstrating how the elements of music are used to achieve unity and variety, tension and release, and balance.

Objective

- Students will demonstrate their knowledge of unity and variety by composing and performing a four-measure phrase using the first five notes of the major scale.

Materials

- Score and recording of the second movement of Haydn's Symphony no. 94 ("Surprise")
- Music for theme from "The Addams Family"
- Audio-playback equipment
- Manuscript paper
- Music example in step 3 on chalkboard
- Overhead projector and transparency with page from the Haydn score (see step 3)

Prior Knowledge and Experiences

- Students have improvised simple melodies and have performed and composed several songs for the right hand using the pitches C to G.

Procedures

1. Review "The Addams Family" theme by playing it on the keyboard for the students.

Ask students to list the measures that are the same.

2. Ask students to assign letters to each measure to illustrate what is the same and what is different (xyy'x).

3. Have students look at the first four measures (or phrase 1) of the second movement of Haydn's "Surprise" Symphony (on the chalkboard).

Ask students to look for similar measures in the music, shown using the overhead projector.

4. Ask students to analyze the repetition and contrast of these measures (xyxz). Discuss how the music is unified and varied.

5. Have students sightread the first four measures of the Haydn theme on keyboards. If pressed for time, have one group of students sightread the first two measures and another group sightread the last two measures. Have students practice playing the music pianissimo and andante. As a surprise, have one group clap, stomp, or drop their books on the floor for the final rest of the phrase.

6. Have students listen to the entire second movement of Haydn's "Surprise" Symphony. Ask students to compare and contrast how the composer unifies the entire work.

7. Ask students to compose and properly notate a four-measure phrase using the pitches C to G and demonstrating repetition and contrast (xyxz). If time allows, have students perform for each other and discuss the use of unity and variety.

(continued)

Indicators of Success

- Students accurately compose, notate on manuscript paper, and perform a phrase demonstrating repetition and contrast.

Follow-up

- Have students create phrases in a similar format using appropriate sound effects found on electronic keyboards.

STANDARD 4C

Composing and arranging music within specified guidelines: Students use a variety of traditional and nontraditional sound sources and electronic media when composing and arranging.

Objective

- Using the pentatonic scale and layered ostinatos, students will create and conduct keyboard ensemble compositions.

Materials

- Electronic keyboards capable of making several sounds (such as vibraphone, harpsichord, and electronic piano) and headsets

- One-measure rhythm cards (all in the same meter) using dotted quarter notes, dotted half notes, and dotted eighth notes

Prior Knowledge and Experiences

- Students can demonstrate independent keyboard performance of rhythms.

- Students can distinguish between two-black-key groups and three-black-key groups.

- Students have been introduced to the pentatonic scale.

- Students are able to conduct in several meters.

Procedures

1. Ask students, with headsets on, to experiment with various rhythm patterns found on the rhythm cards. Have them use black keys only or any pentatonic scale.

2. Divide the class into small groups. Have each group select a rhythm card and create a one-measure ostinato using this rhythm and only black keys. Encourage students to experiment with several pitches.

3. Have each group perform their ostinato pattern for the class. Demonstrate to the class how to create a music composition by layering ostinato patterns. Have each group select a different sound (for example, vibraphone, harpsichord, or electric piano).

4. Demonstrate to the class how to conduct and layer entrances of each group to create a composition. For example, direct Group 1 to begin playing their ostinato and to continue playing until you direct them to stop. After Group 1 plays for two measures, direct Group 2 to begin. Bring in the other groups in like fashion. Have all groups continue playing until you direct them to stop.

5. Have individual students conduct the class composition.

6. Discuss with the class how elements such as tempo, dynamics, octave transposition, and sound (vibraphone, harpsichord, etc.) can affect the composition. Direct the students to experiment with these elements individually and in a group performance.

Indicators of Success

- In the group composition, students perform their independent parts while others are playing.

- Students conduct a group performance.

- Students discuss critically the differences in various compositions.

(continued)

Follow-up

- Have each student create a new composition using ostinatos based on three given one-measure rhythm patterns in a specified meter. Have the students create their own system of notation to communicate to others how they want their composition performed.

- Have students select the "Hit of the Week" composition to be performed by the class.

STANDARD 5A

Reading and notating music: Students read whole, half, quarter, eighth, sixteenth, and dotted notes and rests in 2/4, 3/4, 4/4, 6/8, 3/8, and alla breve meter signatures.

Objective

- Students will read, aurally identify, and perform non-pitched rhythmic lines consisting of whole, half, and quarter notes written in 4/4 meter signature.

Materials

- Guitar, keyboard, or chordal accompaniment instrument
- Teacher-generated rhythm sheets or transparencies (see step 7)
- Overhead projector, if transparencies are used
- Chalkboard
- Notebook paper (optional)

Prior Knowledge and Experiences

- None required.

Procedures

1. Play progressions of eight chords in the key of C as an accompaniment for keeping the beat. Play each chord for four counts, creating eight measures of 4/4 accompaniment (for example, play I, V, I, IV, I, IV, V, I, maintaining each chord for four counts).

2. Have students stamp their feet once (as in o) as each chord change occurs. Then have students snap their fingers twice (as in ♩) for each chord change. Then have students clap their hands four times for each chord change (as in ♩♩♩♩). Repeat until students are adept at each exercise.

3. Repeat step 2, changing stamps, snaps, and claps to three verbal sounds chosen by the students (for example, a sustained hum for the single stamp on each chord change). Have students describe the different durations.

4. Draw a whole note, half note, and quarter note on the chalkboard; then write the words "whole note," "half note," and "quarter note" in a different order. Ask students to match the notes and words. Discuss which represents the stamp (whole note), snap (half note), and clap (quarter note).

5. Ask students to notate the stamp exercise using whole notes. Have volunteers do this at the board, or have students notate at their desks using paper and pencils. Continue this process until students have created eight consecutive whole notes. Give this set of whole notes a name (for example, "Miss Lil's Whole-Note Stomp"). Repeat the process with half notes and quarter notes. Give each of these sets a name.

6. Repeat step 2, telling students to stamp, snap, or clap (or use alternate verbal sounds) according to which type of note is called out prior to the beginning of each chord progression. Ask for volunteers to solo. Use small groups.

7. Show a rhythm sheet consisting of the three 8-measure rhythm exercises used above—all whole notes, all half notes, and all quarter notes—plus five other 8-measure rhythm exercises (with each measure containing all whole, all half, or all quarter notes). Then, ask students to read these rhythm exercises using the procedure introduced in step 2.

(continued)

Indicators of Success

- Students read, aurally identify, and perform a variety of rhythms in 4/4 meter.

Follow-up

- Have students create their own rhythms with combinations of whole, half, and quarter notes; illustrate them on large sheets; and mount them on the walls. Then have student groups read and perform each other's rhythms.

STANDARD 5B

Reading and notating music: Students read at sight simple melodies in both the treble and bass clefs.

Objective

- Students will sightread and aurally identify simple melodic fragments written in the treble and bass clefs.

Materials

- Teacher-generated handouts containing from five to eight short (two- to four-measure) melodic fragments, all in the same key, in treble and bass clefs

- Three additional melodic fragments (on chalkboard or on a transparency) for an in-class demonstration and as an introduction to the activity

- Overhead projector, if transparency is used

- Electronic keyboards and headsets

Prior Knowledge and Experiences

- Students have been introduced to basic note values and note names.

- Students can identify and locate notes of the grand staff at the keyboard.

Procedures

1. Show the students three melodic fragments on the chalkboard or with an overhead projector and transparency. Perform one of the fragments, without identifying which one. Lead the students in a brief discussion of what clues they can use to help them decide which fragment was played (clues such as rhythms used, treble or bass sounds, melodic direction, dynamic levels, and staccato notes). Perform the other two fragments and have students apply these clues.

2. Distribute the handouts of melodic fragments and briefly explain the activity. Have students, using keyboard headsets and working individually or two to a keyboard, sightread the fragments. Explain that, before sightreading each fragment, students should give attention to the same kinds of information they used as clues in step 1 (i.e., rhythms, clef, melodic direction, dynamics, and articulation). Provide assistance as needed and spot check student performances.

3. Have students remove their headsets, and lead them in reading and performing each of the melodic fragments. Have students give small-group performances (for example, three students could play a fragment at the same time) to ensure that all students have an opportunity to perform.

4. After the class has played each of the melodic fragments, ask a few individual students to perform one example of their choice. Ask the other students to use the visual clues discussed previously to identify which examples are played. Repeat this process several times.

Indicators of Success

- Students read and play two- to four-measure melodic fragments at sight.

Follow-up

- Have individual students compose, notate, and play for the class five melodic fragments. Then assign students, at random, to select two or three of these fragments and perform them. Listeners identify the fragments performed.

STANDARD 5C

Reading and notating music: Students identify and define standard notation symbols for pitch, rhythm, dynamics, tempo, articulation, and expression.

Objective

■ Students will demonstrate an understanding of the expressive qualities of music by adding dynamics, articulation, and tempo markings to an existing score.

Materials

■ "One Four Seven," in *Piano for the Developing Musician I,* 3rd ed. (Minneapolis/St. Paul: West Publishing Company, 1993)

Prior Knowledge and Experiences

■ Students have studied the notes of the treble and bass clefs and know keyboard topography.

Procedures

1. Ask students to scan "One Four Seven" and observe the actual number of measures to be learned as well as the pattern of harmonic intervals.

2. Have students block the right- and left-hand intervals, hands together (playing all tones simultaneously), restriking only when the intervals change.

3. Ask students to tap, with both hands, the rhythms of the piece on top of their keyboards, using each hand to tap the rhythm for that particular hand in the piece.

4. Ask half of the class to play the right-hand intervals, as written, while the other half taps the left-hand rhythms, as written, on top of the keyboards. Reverse parts and repeat.

5. Given the meter (8/8), ask students to determine a tempo and write an appropriate musical term to indicate their tempo. Given the overall character of the piece, ask students to determine dynamics and articulation. Have students write appropriate dynamic and articulation markings in their music.

6. Have students play right-hand intervals while tapping left-hand rhythms on top of the keyboards, at the tempo and with the dynamics and articulation they have identified.

7. Have students play both parts of the music expressively as it is now written.

Indicators of Success

■ Students correctly interpret an expanding repertoire of musical markings and symbols in pieces they perform.

Follow-up

■ Have students keep a glossary of musical markings and symbols. This should be an ongoing project with new entries being added each time a new work is studied.

STANDARD 5D

Reading and notating music: Students use standard notation to record their musical ideas and the musical ideas of others.

Objective

- Students will play folk melodies and will notate melodic changes needed to play these melodies based on previously learned scale types (for example, major, minor, blues, whole-tone, and pentatonic).

Materials

- Teacher-generated handouts containing from one to three notated familiar folk melodies (selection of songs to be based on students' current level of keyboard proficiency)

- Electronic keyboards and headsets

- Manuscript paper

Prior Knowledge and Experiences

- Students have constructed and played different scale types (such as major, minor, blues, whole-tone, and pentatonic) on the keyboard or other classroom instruments.

- Students have some experience in writing basic music notation.

Procedures

1. Have students review, write out, and play selected examples of different scale types, including some or all of the major, minor, blues, whole-tone, and pentatonic scales.

2. Distribute the teacher-generated handouts. Have students, using keyboard headsets and working individually or two at a keyboard, practice these melodies on the keyboard. Have students remove headsets and play the melodies as a class or in small groups.

3. Have each student or pair of students, using headsets, choose one of the songs and then play it using a scale type different from the one in which it is written. Have students notate the changes and practice the altered melodies. Do spot checks during this process to see which students need a helping hand.

4. Ask individual students to perform their altered melodies for the class. For some performances, have the students tell which scale types they used; for other performances, have listeners determine which scale type they heard.

Indicators of Success

- Students play the original folk melodies as well as their version of one of these melodies in altered notation that they have written based on a different scale type.

Follow-up

- Select several of the best examples of students' written work and make copies for the class. Consider putting them together to create a class "music book." Have students play selections from their "music book."

STANDARD 5E

Reading and notating music: Students sightread, accurately and expressively, music with a level of difficulty of 2, on a scale of 1 to 6.

Objective

- Students will sightread and play a simple melody with block-chord accompaniment comparable in difficulty to a piece that may be found in a Level 2 piano methods book.

Materials

- Handouts of music for "Go Tell Aunt Rhody" (in key of C)
- Electronic keyboards and headsets

Prior Knowledge and Experiences

- Students know procedures for sightreading.
- Students know the major five-finger patterns of C, G, and F, and the primary triads in the key of C.
- Students have harmonized melodies using simple bass patterns.

Procedures

1. Distribute handouts of music for "Go Tell Aunt Rhody," and have the students sing in unison. Help them analyze the key of the music, the rhythm, and the range of notes.

2. Have the students sightread the melody in C major, as written, in ensemble. Lead the students in reviewing the primary triads in C major and have them play the triads, first with headsets and then in ensemble, as you call out each triad.

3. Play the melody on the keyboard and have students identify the appropriate chord symbols. Have students write the chord symbols on their music.

4. Have the students play the melody in ensemble. Then have them play it with block-chord accompaniment in ensemble.

Indicators of Success

- Students demonstrate their ability to play a simple melody with block-chord accompaniment aurally and expressively.

Follow-up

- On subsequent days, have students follow these steps with many different folk songs to make certain that transfer of learning has taken place.

STANDARD 6C

Listening to, analyzing, and describing music: Students demonstrate knowledge of the basic principles of meter, rhythm, tonality, intervals, chords, and harmonic progressions in their analyses of music.

Objective

- Students will identify and play primary chords of simple folk melodies in C major and G major.

Materials

- *Folk Songs for School and Camp* by Jerry Silverman (Pacific, MO: Mel Bay Publications, 1991), or similar book of folk songs
- Electronic keyboards and headsets

Prior Knowledge and Experiences

- After completing lessons on primary chords in C major and G major, students have compiled a list of folk melodies used at camp, in scouting, or with other groups.
- Students have experience playing simple melodies by ear.

Procedures

1. Perform for the class a familiar folk melody, in C major or G major, using primary chord changes. Ask students to raise their hands when they hear a chord change.

2. Identify the key of the melody. Play the melody once again, having students identify chord changes, calling out the letter name or number of the chord in that key. Ask students to play each of the primary chords.

3. As you play the melody a third time, ask students to play the appropriate chord progression on their keyboards.

4. Have students play the melody by ear with chordal accompaniment.

5. Ask students to each select a folk melody of their choice and to play their melodies, using headsets, with primary chord accompaniment.

6. Ask individual students to perform their melody and chordal accompaniment for the class.

Indicators of Success

- Each student performs for the class a folk melody using primary chord accompaniment.

Follow-up

- Select several students to perform their folk song arrangement while the rest of the class sings.

STANDARD 7A

Evaluating music and music performances: Students develop criteria for evaluating the
quality and effectiveness of music performances and compositions and apply
the criteria in their personal listening and performing.

Objective

■ Students will perform a comparative analysis using correct terminology in discussing various performances of the same musical selection.

Materials

■ Three recordings of Clementi's Sonatina, op. 36, no. 6, performed by three individuals with different levels of ability (the recordings may be of student performances)

■ Audio-playback equipment

■ Teacher-generated handouts showing notation for the main theme of the Sonatina

Prior Knowledge and Experiences

■ Students can aurally identify and correctly label various musical elements: tempo, dynamics, melody, accompaniment, and consonance versus dissonance.

Procedures

1. Play the recording of the least experienced performer and ask the students to pay attention to dynamics, tempo, and melody.

2. After they listen to the recording, ask students to sing the main theme using a neutral syllable such as "la," at the approximate performance tempo and with dynamics and phrasing used in the performance. Have them refer to the notation of the main theme (on the handouts), if necessary.

3. Play the recording of the average-level performer and then have students sing using a neutral syllable at the approximate performance tempo and with dynamics and phrasing used in the performance. Ask questions that focus on a comparison to the first recording played. For example, "Why was this second recording more exciting?" (The dynamics were greater in contrast, and so forth.)

4. Use the same procedure with the recording made by the expert performer. Ask questions that focus on the dynamics, tempo, and shape of the melody. Lead them to recognize that the expert version has a steadier beat (no pauses), the dynamics are more pronounced, and there is better balance between the melody and the accompaniment.

5. Play the recording by the expert performer again. Stop the recording at various locations and call on individuals to verbalize their response to the music. Ask, for example, "What overall effect did the expert performer achieve? What methods did the expert performer use to achieve this effect?" (Accented or unaccented dissonances, ritardando at cadences, maintenance of steady tempo throughout, and so forth)

Indicators of Success

■ Students use appropriate musical vocabulary in describing and comparing musical performances.

Follow-up

- Have students research and bring to class recordings of at least two performances of the same piece of a popular music selection. These two recordings should be of different artists performing the same piece of music. Have students describe, compare, and evaluate these performances using music terminology.

STANDARD 7B

Evaluating music and music performances: Students evaluate the quality and effectiveness of their own and others' performances, compositions, arrangements, and improvisations by applying specific criteria appropriate for the style of the music and offer constructive suggestions for improvement.

Objective

- Students will evaluate and describe their own performance or the performance of others using appropriate music terminology.

Materials

- "Hymn to Freedom," in *Share the Music,* Grade 6 (New York: Macmillan/McGraw-Hill, 1995); or "Lean on Me," in *The Music Connection,* Grade 6 (Parsippany, NJ: Silver Burdett Ginn, 1995), *Music and You,* Grade 6 (New York: Macmillan/McGraw-Hill, 1991), or *Share the Music,* Grade 6

- Student- and teacher-generated list of criteria for performance evaluation (for example, good posture at the piano; correct hand position; relaxed arm, hand, and wrist; correct fingerings, notes, duration of notes, and rhythms; use of correct hand)

Prior Knowledge and Experiences

- Students have been introduced to the components of a successful performance.

- Students have prepared either "Hymn to Freedom" or "Lean on Me" for a class performance.

Procedures

1. Have each student perform his or her piece ("Hymn to Freedom" or "Lean on Me") for the class.

2. Following the performance, ask the performer to name five musical or technical items, from the students' list of criteria for performance evaluation, that were demonstrated in the performance.

3. Following the performer's comments, ask three or four individual students to describe one positive aspect of the performance and something that might be improved in future performances.

Indicators of Success

- The performing student and the listening students correctly identify musical or technical aspects of the performance.

- Students write a brief paragraph describing the musical performance of a class member using musical terminology.

Follow-up

- Ask students to bring prepared piano selections to subsequent classes for evaluative performances.

STANDARD 8A

Understanding relationships between music, the other arts, and disciplines outside the arts:
Students compare in two or more arts how the characteristic materials of each art can be used to transform similar events, scenes, emotions, or ideas into works of art.

Objective

- Students will create music by translating the emotions, theme, and design of a painting into a musical composition.

Materials

- Copy of Paul Klee's painting "Camel in Rhythmical Tree-Landscape"
- Manuscript paper
- Electronic keyboards and headsets

Prior Knowledge and Experiences

- Students have listened to and performed a diverse repertoire of musical compositions and are familiar with visual arts terms.
- Students have discussed how the creative process incorporates meaning, design, and technique.
- Students can notate their compositions using either standard or nonstandard notation.

Procedures

1. Engage students in a discussion describing the camel in Klee's painting. Ask them to study the painting and discuss how the artist uses color, shape, size, line, and spacing to create a visual rhythm.

2. Discuss the kinds of repetition and variety used and their effect on the picture. (Repetition and variety of color, shape, size, and line)

3. Discuss kinds of sounds that could be used to suggest various aspects of the painting. For example, a rising pitch could represent the tree trunk moving upward, or varied dynamics could represent the size and roundness of the tree tops.

4. Having students use headsets at their keyboards, ask them to create their own compositions based on the painting.

5. Ask individual students to play their pieces and to explain why they chose the musical elements evidenced in their piece to describe the theme and design of the painting.

6. Have students notate their compositions so they may be performed by others in the class. Students may choose to use nonstandard notation; however, it must be easily interpreted by the other students.

Indicators of Success

- Students perform a classmate's composition and compare the composition to the painting. They describe the emotions, theme, and design of the painting.

Follow-up

- Find other works of art that will lend themselves to musical interpretation through composition and use a similar procedure with the students.

STANDARD 9A

Understanding music in relation to history and culture: Students describe distinguishing characteristics of representative music genres and styles from a variety of cultures.

Objective

- Students will identify aurally different styles when applied to a common melody and identify aurally what musical element or elements were employed to effect the style change.

Materials

- Electronic keyboard capable of creating both varied sounds and percussion, or recorded/sequenced examples

- Handouts of chart with the headings "Style" and "Describe Elements Used"

- Selected materials explaining the history of language and style, such as *The Music Suite* (Grand Rapids, MI: Yamaha Corporation of America, 1995)

- Recordings of various music selections, including Baroque, Romantic, jazz, Spanish, and African pieces

- Audio-playback equipment

- Student worksheets listing titles of the selected examples (for student descriptions of musical elements in each piece)

Procedures

1. Discuss the English language as representing a standard format that, nonetheless, includes subtle variations in usage. Bring to light how people from different regions of the country speak the same language but with different accents and word choices, for example, "y'all" versus "you all." Lead the students to recognize that different time periods have also affected the way English sounds. Give this example from *The Music Suite*: "Good day, I pray thee, art thou hale and hearty?" can be compared to "Hello, how are you today?" and "Hey! How's it goin'?"

2. Discuss how musical language can be affected by time period and location, resulting in various styles.

3. Have students listen to Baroque, Romantic, jazz, Spanish, and African pieces. On their worksheets, have students describe each piece in terms of the following elements: rhythm, harmony, melody, texture, and form. Then have students discuss the musical elements that make the pieces different from each other.

4. Based on their answers, have the students make some generalized statements about how the treatment of the musical elements affects the style. For example, a Baroque piece may use a harpsichord while a jazz piece may use a piano or organ (texture). Improvisation is present in both jazz and Baroque, but the form is different.

5. Distribute handouts of chart. Play "Twinkle, Twinkle, Little Star" in a basic style with no additional instruments or accompaniment. Then play the song on electronic keyboard in the following styles (or play recorded/sequenced examples): Baroque (using arpeggiated accompaniment with harpsichord), Romantic (using violin as melody and playing in a legato style), jazz (playing melody with swing bass or rhythm section), Spanish (using nylon guitar string sound as well as castanets from the drum sounds), and African (playing melody across talking drum sounds). For each example, have students write down the style and identify which elements of music (rhythm, harmony, melody, texture, or form) were used to create that style.

6. Discuss the students' answers with them, focusing on the musical elements that make the style of each piece distinctive.

Prior Knowledge and Experiences

- Students have an understanding of the characteristics of various musical time periods and styles, such as Classical, jazz, Romantic, Baroque, Spanish, and African.

Indicators of Success

- Students demonstrate their understanding of different styles in their answers written on their worksheets.

Follow-up

- Assign a simple song for students to play and then modify through stylistic changes. Have them explain what they did and why, identifying the particular style they had in mind.

- Expand styles under study to include spirituals, folk songs, protest songs, and so forth.

STANDARD 9C

Understanding music in relation to history and culture: Students compare, in several cultures of the world, functions music serves, roles of musicians, and conditions under which music is typically performed.

Objective

■ Students will describe the similarities and differences in the roles of keyboard musicians in different societies.

Materials

■ None required

Prior Knowledge and Experiences

■ Students are familiar with such genres as Bach organ works, Scarlatti or Couperin harpsichord/clavichord pieces, and Liszt or Debussy piano pieces, as well as music of contemporary keyboard artists such as Yanni, Paul Schaefer, Billy Joel, and Herbie Hancock.

■ Students have been assigned to work in groups of three, with one student in each group assigned to research the music of a keyboard artist in each of the past three centuries (eighteenth, nineteenth, and twentieth). They have been asked to consider the music (why and for whom it was written and played), how the composer/performer made a living, and what a typical performance situation would involve (including the keyboard instrument used).

Procedures

1. Have the students meet in their groups and compare their findings about the music of various keyboard artists.

2. Have students prepare a presentation (oral report, class demonstration, or written report) demonstrating the similarities and differences in the subjects and their time periods.

3. If students are at a high enough performance level, designate one student in each group as the "player" who will perform a short excerpt of the music under study.

Indicators of Success

■ Students demonstrate an awareness of the changing roles of musicians, from church- or court-supported artists to teacher/salon artists performing for the aristocracy to twentieth-century concert/media artists.

■ Students describe the changes in keyboard instruments over the centuries as well as the changes in compositional style.

Follow-up

■ Arrange a collaborative effort within the arts that might result in an original production, complete with period costumes, music, and dance. Devise an appropriate title, such as "The Bs: Bach to Brahms to Billy Joel."

STRATEGIES
Grades 9–12

STANDARD 1C

Singing, alone and with others, a varied repertoire of music:
Students demonstrate well-developed ensemble skills.

Objective

- Students will sing and play a selection with accurate pitches and rhythm while demonstrating ensemble skills such as balance of dynamics and proper pedaling.

Materials

- "Lullay, Thou Little Tiny Child," in *Piano: Classic Themes,* Level 4, from *Alfred's Basic Piano Library* (Van Nuys, CA: Alfred Publishing Company, 1990)
- Electronic keyboards, headsets, and speakers

Prior Knowledge and Experiences

- Students have learned to sing "Lullay, Thou Little Tiny Child" and can sing it from memory.

Procedures

1. Ask students to listen as you play through the score of "Lullay, Thou Little Tiny Child." Play it a second time while students sing.

2. With the keyboards on "speaker," have students play the left hand of the score using the pedal indicated in the score. Have them repeat the left-hand part as you play the right-hand part. Repeat again, asking students to pay particular attention to the indicated dynamics.

3. With the keyboards on "headset," have students work through the suggested fingering for the right hand. Ask students which harmonic intervals are prevalent. (Sixths and thirds)

4. Place students in duet pairs and have one student in each pair play bass clef while the other plays treble clef. Have students switch parts and repeat this.

5. Select "accompanist" teams from the duet pairs and let various teams play, one team at a time, as other students sing.

6. Have a class performance, with all students playing "accompaniment duets" and singing at the same time, paying particular attention to performing well as an ensemble. Balance and appropriate dynamic levels, as well as proper pedaling, are critical to the success of the collaboration.

Indicators of Success

- As students accompany their singing, they perform pitches and rhythms accurately and demonstrate ensemble skills such as good balance of dynamic levels and matching pedaling.

Follow-up

- Have individual students play "Lullay, Thou Little Tiny Child" as written (as a solo piano composition).

STANDARD 2A

Performing on instruments, alone and with others, a varied repertoire of music:
Students perform with expression and technical accuracy a large and varied repertoire
of instrumental literature with a level of difficulty of 4, on a scale of 1 to 6.

Objective

■ Students will demonstrate legato articulation as an expressive quality in performing keyboard literature from a Level 4 piano methods book.

Materials

■ "Spanish Guitars," in *Piano*, Level 4, from *Bastien Piano Basics* (San Diego: Neil A. Kjos Music Company, 1985)

■ Recording of a guitarist strumming notes as well as playing melodically

■ Audio-playback equipment

Prior Knowledge and Experiences

■ Students have developed good music reading skills and have been introduced to the use of the pedal.

Procedures

1. Have students listen to a recording or a live performance of a guitarist strumming notes as well as playing melodically.

2. Ask students to do a rhythmic analysis of the composition and discuss the differences between rhythms in 6/8 and 3/4 meter signatures and their relationship to the mood of the composition.

3. Have students analyze the composition "Spanish Guitars" harmonically and identify the melodic ideas. Discuss with students the compositional techniques used by the composer to create a feeling of guitars in this piece (use of arpeggios to give a feeling of strumming as on a guitar).

4. Demonstrate staccato and legato styles of playing arpeggios. Have students practice playing arpeggios staccato and then legato.

5. As students practice this composition, urge them to think about the sound of the guitar being strummed as well as the guitar as a solo instrument. Have students work both with and without the pedal.

6. If possible, have students record their practice and listen to the tape or disk for self-analysis. Ask students to critique each other during class performances, and offer your own analysis as appropriate.

Indicators of Success

■ During student performances for peer evaluations, students demonstrate the expressive qualities of the music, particularly legato articulation.

Follow-up

■ Assign additional repertoire pieces representing other instruments. The pieces could include sheet music, such as Olson's "Blazing Trumpets" (Van Nuys, CA: Alfred Publishing Company, 1986); Jerrould's "Hornpipe" (Cincinnati: Willis Music Company, 1985); Vandall's "Pianist on the Prowl" (Boulder, CO: Myklas Music Press, 1985); Ehrhardt's "Prelude: Song of the Harp" (Cincinnati: Willis Music Company, 1984); or Burnam's "Two Flutes a-Fluting" (Cincinnati: Willis Music Company, 1983). Or, the pieces could include music from methods books, such as "Highland Tune," in *Piano Discoveries C,* from *Music Pathways* (New York: Carl Fischer, 1983); "Old Fiddle Tune," in *Piano Discoveries B,* from *Music Pathways*; "Reveille," in *Piano,* Level 3, from *Bastien Piano Basics* (San Diego: Neil A. Kjos Music Company, 1985); or "Swiss Music Box," in *Piano,* Level 4, from *Bastien Piano Basics.*

STANDARD 2B

Performing on instruments, alone and with others, a varied repertoire of music: Students perform an appropriate part in an ensemble, demonstrating well-developed ensemble skills.

Objective

- Students will perform duets with particular attention to musical elements, such as rhythm, chords, melodic design, octave registers, and correct finger action.

Materials

- "Calico Rag," in *Chord Approach Duet Book,* Level 1, from *Alfred's Basic Piano Library* (Van Nuys, CA: Alfred Publishing Company, 1987)
- Electronic keyboards and headsets

Prior Knowledge and Experiences

- Students have learned basic music fundamentals, keyboard topography, octave registers, major and minor chords, and basic note values.

Procedures

1. Have students, working individually or in pairs, learn each part of the duet. Ask them to think about the composition in terms of such elements as rhythm, melodic design, chord functions (major/minor), and octave registers. (In some classes, you may elect to have students learn and perform Primo only, as you play Secondo.)

2. Have students identify melodic and rhythmic patterns in each part of the duet.

3. Direct students to work in pairs and have one student clap the rhythm of the melody while the other claps the harmonic rhythm prior to rehearsing the composition at the keyboard using headsets.

4. As students rehearse together, have them identify melodic patterns or ideas, as well as the major and minor chord structure of the composition. You could give a tape recording or sequencer disk of the practice session to each student for study at home.

5. Have pairs of students play the duet for the class at a tempo comfortable for them.

6. Have other members of the piano class critique the performance of the duet, focusing on rhythmic accuracy, balance between parts, and fingering technique.

Indicators of Success

- Pairs of students perform the duet in a musical manner, using correct notes, rhythm, and proper technique, as evidenced by the critiques of the other students and their own analysis of their performance.

Follow-up

- Have students perform and/or compose varied duets of their choice.

STANDARD 2C

Performing on instruments, alone and with others, a varied repertoire of music: Students perform in small ensembles with one student on a part.

Objective

■ Students will perform any part of a four-part keyboard ensemble with musical sensitivity in a "hard rock" style.

Materials

■ "Rast's Roost," in *Jam Session* (Milwaukee: Hal Leonard Corporation, 1993)

■ Drum machine or drum set (optional)

Prior Knowledge and Experiences

■ Students can read single line parts in either the treble or bass clef on the keyboard.

■ Students have studied syncopation and have improvised melodies using the C blues scale.

Procedures

1. Have students analyze Part 4 of "Rast's Roost" and help them discover the use of pattern, repetition, and sequence (the repetition of a pattern beginning on a different pitch). Have them clap the rhythm observing the accents. Have them analyze suggested fingering.

2. Ask students to "play" Part 4 on a closed keyboard cover, observing correct rhythm, accents, fingering, and approximate pitches. Then ask them to play the music on the keyboard. You, or students with previous keyboard experience, may add Parts 2 and 3. Determine an appropriate "hard rock" tempo.

3. Have students analyze Parts 2 and 3 in the same way that they analyzed Part 4. Encourage them to create several different comping rhythms (patterns of regularly and irregularly spaced chords that punctuate and complement the melody) that enhance Part 4. Encourage individual students to try their rhythm while a peer plays Part 4. Have students take turns playing Parts 2, 3, and 4. Encourage an effective balance between the three parts.

4. Have students analyze Part 1 to discover the use of pattern, repetition, rhythmic variation, and syncopation. Ask students to clap the rhythm observing accents. Have all students play Part 1 through measure 25. Ask students to discuss appropriate balance (should Part 1 be strongest?) and then ask assigned students to add Parts 2, 3, and 4 through measure 25.

5. Review the C blues scale, focusing on the blue notes (lowered 3rd, 5th, and 7th). Students lacking technical facility may use the first five notes of the scale.

6. Have individuals take turns improvising a melody while a specified group of students play Parts 2, 3, and 4 (one student on each part). Have students perform the complete ensemble, switching parts as desired. Add an appropriate drum machine (or drum set) accompaniment.

(continued)

Indicators of Success

- Students successfully perform any part of "Rast's Roost" musically, observing effective melodic balance. They comp rhythms that enhance the ensemble and improvise melodies using the C blues scale.

Follow-up

- Assign additional selections from *Jam Session* or other appropriate ensemble materials that use multiple parts with suggested improvisation.

STANDARD 2D

Performing on instruments, alone and with others, a varied repertoire of music:
Students perform with expression and technical accuracy a large and varied repertoire of instrumental literature with a level of difficulty of 5, on a scale of 1 to 6.

Objective

- Students will perform an advanced ensemble piece with expression and technical accuracy on multiple keyboards or with percussion accompaniment.

Materials

- "Dance to It!" in *Originals* from *Ogilvy Keyboard Multiples,* Book 1 (Denton, TX: Ogilvy Music, 1991)
- Electronic keyboards and headsets
- Audiocassette recorder, microphone (or patch cord), and blank tape
- Drum set and student drummer (optional)

Prior Knowledge and Experiences

- Some students have experience reading more than one part from the open score of a multikeyboard work.
- Some students have knowledge of and experience with syncopation as well as elementary experience with sequencing sounds.

Procedures

1. Ask students to study the whole score and determine which of the six parts are similar. (Parts 1 and 2; Parts 3 and 5)

2. Have students notice changes that occur at the main cadences (activity will usually increase at these points).

3. Have students, while counting out loud, tap the rhythm of Part 4, paying particular attention to the second half of beat three. If a drum set and drummer are available, have the students count and tap Part 4 again as the drummer plays Part 6.

4. Assign parts to students and ask them to practice their parts with headsets on. Have them consider the following sound settings from the composers: "Parts 1 and 2 could be played by one player and doubled as much as desired with multiple sound settings for fullness and effect. Experiment with various synth timbres. Parts 1 and 2 should have shimmering effects while Part 3 should be more sustained. Part 4 should be a punchy analogue sound with Part 5 being the carpet. Sound should change at letter C to more subtle sounds, building to measure 37, then changing back to original sound at letter A" (from notes by Jim and Susan Ogilvy).

5. Have students do repeated rehearsals with particular attention to rhythmic accuracy and expressiveness. Peer and teacher input (assessment) is essential for continued improvement.

6. Have students tape their performance of the piece and then play it back for self-evaluation, paying particular attention to rhythmic and technical accuracy.

Indicators of Success

- Students demonstrate the ability to cooperate musically and technically within an ensemble performance and perform with expression and technical accuracy.

Follow-up

- Have jazz band members (saxophonists, trumpeters, etc.) in the class use chord progression sheets to improvise melodic material as the keyboard ensemble performs the piece.

STANDARD 3A

Improvising melodies, variations, and accompaniments: Students improvise stylistically appropriate harmonizing parts.

Objective

- Students will create and improvise appropriate harmonizing parts based upon a lead sheet chord symbol analysis of a repertoire piece.

Materials

- Scherzo, op. 39, no. 12, by Kabalevsky

Prior Knowledge and Experiences

- Students can recognize and play white-key triads in root position, blocked and arpeggiated (specifically, C, Dm, Em, F, G, Am, and B dim).

- Students can play literature, such as that found in a Level 2 piano methods book.

Procedures

1. Have students analyze Kabalevsky's scherzo. Help them discover the use of pattern, repetition, sequence, and rhythmic variation. Have them note how the pattern in the first measure is treated sequentially throughout.

2. Guide students to discover that Kabalevsky uses only white-key triads in the root position. Analyze each triad using lead sheet chord symbols and write the symbols above the staff.

3. Have students read the piece playing the triads as block chords rather than arpeggiated, as written.

4. Have students play the piece as written, observing articulations, dynamic contrasts, and tempo indications.

5. Using the scherzo as a style model, encourage students to create a one-measure harmonic figure using block and/or arpeggiated triads (repetitive rhythmic treatment of the triad in either block or broken style). Then, using the lead sheet chord symbols as a guide, have students improvise a new harmonic accompaniment to the scherzo based on the one-measure harmonic figure created.

6. Allow each student to play his or her improvised harmonization while several other students play the piece as originally written.

7. Discuss with students which harmonizations were most effective and why (octave placement, creative use of blocked and/or arpeggiated chords, balance, dynamic contrasts).

Indicators of Success

- Each student successfully improvises and plays his or her new harmonization of the Kabalevsky scherzo.

Follow-up

- Changing the initial lead sheet chord symbol to G (from C), help students discover the root-position triads to be used. Ask if they are all white-key triads. (No. They are G, Am, Bm, C, D, Em, and F-sharp dim.) Repeat the same exercise as above.

STANDARD 3B

Improvising melodies, variations, and accompaniments: Students improvise rhythmic and melodic variations on given pentatonic melodies and melodies in major and minor keys.

Objective

- Students will improvise a simple melody and then create rhythmic, melodic, and harmonic variations based on a given melody.

Materials

- Manuscript paper and/or chalkboard
- Handouts with notation of melody for "Twinkle, Twinkle, Little Star"

Prior Knowledge and Experiences

- Students have performed all major and minor pentascales, hands together, and can identify tonic, subdominant, and dominant tones of the scale.
- Students have been introduced to question-and-answer phrases.

Procedures

1. Have students choose a "key of the day." Have them warm up by playing the pentascale of this key, hands together.

2. Have students identify the I, IV, and V tones of the key and have them play the single tones in the left hand.

3. Divide students into groups and have each decide on the length and meter of a melody to be improvised. Have each student either write or play a melody within the parameters identified by his or her group and in the key of the day. Remind students of the importance of phrase structure.

4. Ask each student to play his or her melody for the class. Ask each student, on a second playing, to add a single-tone harmony to the melody, using the I, IV, and V tones of the key of the day.

5. Play the melody of "Twinkle, Twinkle, Little Star" and then play two short variations of this familiar tune. Discuss theme-and-variation form and ways to create variations. For example, play the song and embellish the melody; then play the song and create a different rhythmic structure. Ask students to describe some of the variations they have heard.

6. Distribute handouts with melody notation for "Twinkle." Assign each student a type of variation to improvise: rhythmic, melodic, or harmonic. Have students improvise their variations while using handouts. Then have students notate their improvised variations.

7. Ask individual students to play their improvisation for the class. Have the class identify how the student created the variation.

Indicators of Success

- Students discriminate the ways a melody, rhythm, or harmony can be varied. Students perform individual variations and demonstrate their understanding of improvisation and variation.

Follow-up

- Students select favorite folk melodies to use as the basis for further improvisation in the variation genre.

STANDARD 3C

Improvising melodies, variations, and accompaniments: Students improvise original melodies over given chord progressions, each in a consistent style, meter, and tonality.

Objective

- Students will create and improvise melodies over given accompaniment patterns.

Materials

- A series of short action scenarios, rich in possible detail and ambiguous in meaning, such as "Walking down a dark street late at night," "A rough trip through the Deep Space Nine wormhole," and "Downhill skiing through an alpine forest" (scenarios with a beginning, middle, and end that last no more than five minutes)
- Electronic keyboards and headsets
- Chalkboard

Prior Knowledge and Experiences

- Students have created melodic and harmonic improvisations for given melodies.

Procedures

1. Write a scenario (see ideas in Materials), no longer than one or two sentences, on a chalkboard easily seen at a glance from the keyboards.
2. Briefly discuss the scenario with students, pointing out key words that suggest an expressive approach.
3. Establish guidelines for the scenario (for example, tonal center or rhythmic or melodic motif).
4. Give students a few minutes of private exploration (using headsets) to develop their sounds and improvisational ideas for each section of the scenario.
5. Play an accompaniment pattern while leading the ensemble through the scenario, using conducting techniques, hand gestures, and verbal suggestions and encouragement. When a strong motif emerges, encourage students to respond to it appropriately. Allow the improvisational composition to emerge, but move the group ahead if they get stuck on one idea or theme. Listen for an appropriate end. Create one if necessary.
6. Encourage students to notate any themes they find especially appealing or interesting and incorporate them into a more formal composition.

Indicators of Success

- Students create improvisations over given accompaniment patterns.

Follow-up

- Ask all students to submit scenarios. Explain that two will be chosen for a class project resulting in two one-act plays, complete with original dialogue, sets, and music.

STANDARD 3E

Improvising melodies, variations, and accompaniments: Students improvise original melodies in a variety of styles, over given chord progressions, each in a consistent style, meter, and tonality.

Objective

- Students will improvise a melody over a given chord progression, retaining the original style and meter.

Materials

- Compositions (in a major key) from keyboard repertoire
- Electronic keyboards and headsets

Prior Knowledge and Experiences

- Students are knowledgeable about the characteristics of the natural minor scale and can perform this scale.

Procedures

1. After reviewing a short section of a composition written in a major key, lead the students in a discussion of the qualities of the parallel minor key.

2. Have students perform the parallel natural minor scale to the given major key of the composition.

3. Have students, using headsets, re-create the written composition at the keyboard, using the natural minor key. Ask students to discuss the performance reflecting the key change.

4. Ask students to keep the original harmony in the minor key and improvise a similar stylistic melody over it.

5. Lead the students in a discussion of the effect of modality and key choices on their improvisation.

Indicators of Success

- Students stay within the natural minor scale form and improvise a similar stylistic melody over the harmony given.

Follow-Up

- Ask students to improvise in a blues style, using a set twelve-bar harmonic progression and melodic material from a blues penta-scale. Have students use a digital sequencer to program background accompaniments.

STANDARD 4A

Composing and arranging music within specified guidelines: Students compose music in several distinct styles, demonstrating creativity in using the elements of music for expressive effect.

Objective

- Students will compose a short descriptive miniature—a composition that uses music to "paint" a picture.

Materials

- "Dripping Faucet" by Alan Shulman, in *Piano for the Developing Musician 1,* 3rd ed. (Minneapolis/St. Paul: West Publishing Company, 1993)
- Electronic keyboards and headsets

Prior Knowledge and Experiences

- Students have experience composing and performing original works in the style of repertoire studied, in ABA form with B section modulation, and using theme and variation.

Procedures

1. Play "Dripping Faucet" for the students without telling them the name of the composition. Ask students what the music makes them think about.

2. After telling students the title of the composition, ask them what other objects or events could be the basis of a good descriptive miniature (for example, a passing parade, a video game, a traffic jam, a persistent alarm clock, an argument between two people, or a carousel).

3. Have students, with headsets on, experiment with keyboard sounds to illustrate various objects or events.

4. Have the students form several groups. Direct each group to create a descriptive miniature (of eight to sixteen measures) and then select a performer from within the group to play the miniature. Encourage each group to consider the creative use of the elements of music.

5. Ask the selected performers to play their group's miniature and let the rest of the class try to guess the title. Have them discuss what musical elements help to convey that idea to the listeners.

Indicators of Success

- Students create a short composition to portray a particular object, sound, mood, or happening.

Follow-up

- Ask individual students to compose a descriptive miniature and then select several miniatures for classroom performance.

STANDARD 4B

Composing and arranging music within specified guidelines: *Students arrange pieces for voices or instruments other than those for which the pieces were written in ways that preserve or enhance the expressive effect of the music.*

Objective

- Students will orchestrate and perform a composition in four or more parts using a variety of techniques and timbres.

Materials

- Any hymn or chorale written in four-part chordal style
- Electronic keyboards capable of making a variety of sounds or other sound modules with prerecorded sounds

Prior Knowledge and Experiences

- Students can read and play single-line notation using either the treble clef or the bass clef at the keyboard.

Procedures

1. Have students analyze the hymn (or chorale) and divide the lines into four separate parts, usually called soprano, alto, tenor, and bass.

2. With students working four to a group, have each student in the group orchestrate one of the four parts of the composition.

3. Ask each group to select a timbre for each part (for example, harpsichord, strings, organ, vibraphone, or trumpet).

4. Have each group select a different hymn or chorale and create a multiple-keyboard arrangement. This one could be for string sextet or quartet with trumpet and vibes, or any combination of instrumental sounds available to the students. Encourage them to explore the use of doubling of parts and octave transposition, as well as solo passages or other expressive elements.

5. Have each group of students perform their orchestration for the class and discuss their reasons for making the decisions used in creating their work.

Indicators of Success

- Using a variety of timbres and techniques, students orchestrate and then perform their pieces.

Follow-up

- Have students create orchestrations using chamber or full orchestra styles of orchestration.
- Have students study one of the selections in *Baroque Mix* by Dawn Miller (San Diego, CA: Neil A. Kjos Music Company, 1990).

STANDARD 4C

Composing and arranging music within specified guidelines: Students compose and arrange music for voices and various acoustic and electronic instruments, demonstrating knowledge of the ranges and traditional usages of the sound sources.

Objective

- Students will create modal vocal pieces consisting of a vocal line and a simple keyboard accompaniment.

Materials

- Texts of the poems "The Panther" and "The Pizza" by Ogden Nash (from any edition of Nash's poems or collected works)

Prior Knowledge and Experiences

- Students are familiar with the modes built on each tone of the major scale.

- Students have experience with a variety of chordal accompaniment figures such as block chords, broken chords, Alberti bass, and two-handed accompaniment.

Procedures

1. Ask individual students to read each of the Ogden Nash poems and to emphasize the syllabic rhythm as they read. Tell students that they will be creating pieces using these texts. Stress to students the importance of melodic and harmonic (through accompaniment) reinforcement of the syllabic emphasis of the text.

2. Have students review the following modes: C Dorian (from C to C with the key signature of B-flat major), G Lydian (from G to G with the key signature of D major), and G Locrian (from G to G with the key signature of A-flat major).

3. Have students choose one of the two poems to serve as the basis for a new piece. Ask students to create a piece consisting of a vocal line and a simple accompaniment. For students choosing "The Panther," assign the C Dorian mode. For those choosing "The Pizza," assign a combination of G Lydian and G Locrian.

4. Have students work in small groups or in pairs to create vocal and keyboard compositions using their chosen poem and the assigned modes.

5. Ask student volunteers to perform their pieces. Have them explain their reasons for choosing certain sounds for the melodic and harmonic reinforcement.

Indicators of Success

- Several student volunteers perform their pieces and describe to the class why they chose certain sounds for the melodic and harmonic reinforcement.

Follow-up

- Ask all students to give classroom performances of their compositions. Allow them adequate rehearsal time for both the keyboard and the voice parts.

STANDARD 5B

Reading and notating music: Students sightread, accurately and expressively, music with a level of difficulty of 3, on a scale of 1 to 6.

Objective

- From a source comparable to a Level 3 piano methods book, students will sightread duet pieces based on the A natural minor scale.

Materials

- "Song I" and "Song II," in *One Plus One* (Van Nuys, CA: Alfred Publishing Company, 1986)
- Electronic keyboards

Prior Knowledge and Experiences

- Students are at the early-to-middle intermediate level in their keyboard skills.

Procedures

1. Have students determine the range of the right hand in "Song I." (An octave)

2. Ask students to compare the range of the right hand in "Song I" to the range of the right hand in "Song II." Are they similar? (Yes, however, for the first eight measures of "Song II" there is an octavo marking.) Have students define "loco." (Return to the octave in which the music is written.) Ask them where "Song I" uses an octavo marking.

3. Have students determine what two harmonic intervals are used in the left hand of "Song I." (Fifth and sixth)

4. Have students compare the intervals of the left hand in both songs. ("Song I" uses two harmonic intervals; "Song II" uses one melodic interval.)

5. If students are in a piano lab situation, divide the class evenly and assign half to sightread "Song I" and the other half to sightread "Song II." If the control center has a "pair" button, allow students to work on the ensemble as a team, one performing "Song I" and the other, "Song II."

6. Have students perform as two-part ensembles in groups of four students at a time.

Indicators of Success

- Students work as teams and sightread accurately and expressively assigned "Song I" or "Song II" as solos.

Follow-up

- Choose other solos or duets from this collection or other collections for work in class or outside of class. Have students perform similar activities in major keys.

STANDARD 5D

Reading and notating music: Students interpret nonstandard notation symbols used by some twentieth-century composers.

Objective

- Students will interpret and perform a piece by a 20th-century composer.

Materials

- "Middle, Bottom, and Top" by Ross Lee Finney, in *Mosaics* (Orem, UT: Sonos Music Resources, 1973)
- Grand piano

Prior Knowledge and Experiences

- Students have a working knowledge of ledger lines.

Procedures

1. Ask students to list what they consider to be the common elements of music that might be used in a composition. (Sound: pitch, duration, timbre, dynamics, texture, form; silence: duration)

2. To experiment with sound, have students pluck the strings inside the piano. Have one student pluck the strings for the lowest key, and then have another student pluck the strings for the highest key. What is the difference?

3. Have students determine the meaning for *p, sfz, f, pp, mf, 15ma* (two octaves higher than written), and *8va*. Explain that the composer of "Middle, Bottom, and Top" has given the following explanation for the V marks: "a pause of indeterminate length, and the beams on the repeated high C—the duration will get slower as they go from 32nd notes to eighth notes."

4. Because there are no meter signature or bar lines given in the music, have students discuss the element of duration in this piece.

5. Have student volunteers perform this work.

Indicators of Success

- Students let their own interpretation influence the performance of music using nonstandard notation.

Follow-up

- Have students compose a piece of music using nonstandard notation. Explain that the use of a staff is not mandatory.

STANDARD 6C

Listening to, analyzing, and describing music: Students identify and explain compositional devices and techniques used to provide unity and variety and tension and release in a musical work and give examples of other works that make similar uses of these devices and techniques.

Objective

- Students will analyze and describe devices used to cause tension and release in a given piano piece.

Materials

- "Toreador," in *Miniatures, Book 3* (Boston: Galaxy Music, 1964; distributed by ECS Publishing)

Prior Knowledge and Experiences

- Students have done extensive work with intervals, penta-scales, and root-position triads.

Procedures

1. Ask students to scan the score of "Toreador" and observe the use of root-position triads. What is their primary function? (Harmonic accompaniment)

2. Ask students to observe the use of broken triads. What is their primary function? (Melodic material)

3. Play "Toreador" for the class.

4. Have students determine the reason for the meter changes. (They are used to heighten the impending musical climax of measure 19.)

5. Ask for a volunteer to explain the picture painted by "Toreador." Does the bull win? How does the composer use chord changes and accents for tension and release?

6. Play the piece again, having the students listen particularly for the devices and techniques they have identified.

Indicators of Success

- Students analyze and discuss devices and techniques used to cause tension and release in the music.

Follow-up

- Ask students to help compile a list of works that make similar use of these compositional devices and techniques to provide unity and variety and tension and release. The list could begin with "Flickering Candle" by Lynn Freeman Olson, in *Piano for the Developing Musician I,* 3rd ed. (Minneapolis/St. Paul: West Publishing Company, 1993).

STANDARD 6F

Listening to, analyzing, and describing music: Students analyze and describe uses of the elements of music in a given work that make it unique, interesting, and expressive.

Objective

- Students will analyze, describe, and perform, with their own interpretation, a work using nonstandard notation.

Materials

- "Inner View" by Lynn Freeman Olson, in *Piano for the Developing Musician I,* 3rd ed. (Minneapolis/St. Paul: West Publishing Company, 1993)

Prior Knowledge and Experiences

- Students have studied major and minor pentascales, ledger lines, basic articulations, and preliminary pedal technique.

Procedures

1. Have students notice the absence of a meter signature or bar lines in "Inner View." What should this mean to the performer?

2. Ask students to determine the overall pitch range of the piece and the overall dynamic range of the piece.

3. Ask for volunteers to perform "Inner View." Have students discuss the individual interpretations of the piece. How do the interpretations differ? How are they similar? What musical elements did the performers emphasize to make the piece unique, interesting, and expressive?

Indicators of Success

- Students describe, analyze, and play the piece with variety and accuracy.

Follow-up

- Have students compose a piece in the style of "Inner View." Have students trade compositions for performance.

STANDARD 7B

Evaluating music and music performances: Students evaluate a performance, composition, arrangement, or improvisation by comparing it to similar or exemplary models.

Objective

- Students will identify aurally prominent musical concepts when listening to music and compare various performances of the same piece.

Materials

- Three recordings of Beethoven's Sonata, op. 53, in C Major ("Waldstein"), performed by three different individuals
- Audio-playback equipment
- Chalkboard

Prior Knowledge and Experiences

- Students have identified and categorized various aspects of performances: tempo, dynamics, timbre, accompaniment, consonant versus dissonant sounds, and rhythm.

Procedures

1. List on the board prominent musical concepts and aspects such as dynamics, timbre, accompaniment, consonant versus dissonant sounds, and rhythm. Play one recorded performance of the exposition of the Beethoven sonata.

2. Ask the students to write down which of the concepts or aspects they noticed when listening to the piece.

3. Play the same excerpt from the second recorded performance. Ask the students to compare the items noted from the first performance with the same items in the second performance.

4. Have students note, in writing, any new aspects.

5. Have students listen to the third recorded performance. Follow the same procedure as above.

6. Following all performances and responses, ask various individuals which performance was faster. Did the faster tempo make the piece more exciting for the listener? Did it make the piece unsettling for the listener? Did the tempo change the rhythmic steadiness? Is rhythmic steadiness an important aspect of this piece?

7. Since these exact issues may not be the aspects addressed by the students, play the first twenty-four measures of each recording again. Then, ask students to write answers to each of the questions in step 6.

Indicators of Success

- Students respond in a thoughtful and meaningful manner to each of the questions. Students become more aware of performance skills.

Follow-up

- Have students discuss which aspects of the performances of the Beethoven sonata will help them focus on improving their own performance skills.

STANDARD 8A

Understanding relationships between music, the other arts, and disciplines outside the arts:
*Students explain how elements, artistic processes, and organizational principles are used
in similar and distinctive ways in the various arts and cite examples.*

Objective

- Students will compare and contrast character development in a literary work and a musical composition.

Materials

- "The Old Man and the Sea" by Ernest Hemingway
- "Hero" by Walter Afanasieff and Mariah Carey (New York: Sony Music Publishing, 1993)

Prior Knowledge and Experiences

- Students have studied "The Old Man and the Sea" in their English literature class (as part of a correlation lesson with music class).
- Students can play "Hero" on the keyboard.

Procedures

1. Discuss with the class the development of Santiago's character and his relationship with Manuel, the boy, in "The Old Man and the Sea." Point out similarities in this relationship to that of Santiago's admiration for Joe DiMaggio. Also, note the need for heroes or role models in society.

2. Have students play "Hero" together on their keyboards. Ask the class: "What musical effects did the composers use to convey feelings toward the hero?" (Rise and fall of melodic line, octave leap in the bass line followed by slow-moving, descending, chromatic bass line, etc.)

3. Assign students to write an essay that compares and contrasts Hemingway's character development of Santiago with Afanasieff and Carey's "Hero." (Some points of comparison to consider might be similarities of both works in describing a hero as strong in character. The literary work also describes the physical strength of the hero in words while the musical work implies physical strength through increase in dynamics.)

Indicators of Success

- Students develop and write a comparison/contrast essay that deals with issues raised in the class discussion.

Follow-up

- Have students find other songs about a hero and compare/contrast them to Santiago's admiration for Joe DiMaggio.

STANDARD 9C

Understanding music in relation to history and culture: Students identify various roles that musicians perform, cite representative individuals who have functioned in each role, and describe their activities and achievements.

Objective

- Students will write about various career options in music, discuss these careers with classmates, and summarize the music careers of three well-known performers.

Materials

- Chalkboard
- Music journals (maintained by the students as part of their class work)

Prior Knowledge and Experiences

- Students have listened to recorded interviews with three professional musicians. For example, "Dave Brubeck Interview," "Wynton Marsalis Interview," and "Dolly Parton Interview," all from *The Music Connection,* Grade 8, CD Library (Parsippany, NJ: Silver Burdett Ginn, 1995).

Procedures

1. Ask the students to pretend that they are planning to become one of the following: piano maker, rock star, opera singer, recording technician, music arranger for a country-western star, orchestra conductor, band director in a high school, or music teacher in a middle school.

2. Write the list on the chalkboard. Ask for student input for any other music careers that could be added to the list.

3. Ask students to select a career and to consider these questions: How can you learn what you will need to know to pursue a career in music? What sort of education will you need to pursue your chosen career? How much musical knowledge will you need? How will you let a prospective employer know that you are qualified for a certain type of work?

4. Ask students to write their answers in outline form in their music journals. Help students as needed.

5. Ask for volunteers to present their outlines to the class.

Indicators of Success

- Students write thoughtful entries about career options in music in their journals. Students share their thoughts and concerns in class discussions.

(continued)

Follow-up

- Ask students to write summaries of the interviews they listened to in class (i.e., the Brubeck, Marsalis, and Parton interviews). Ask students to formulate questions they would like to ask famous musicians if given a chance—questions about achieving a successful career in music.

- Have students, working in groups, identify local pianists and keyboard players for possible interviews. Have the students report on the results of their findings. Invite those local artists who agreed to be interviewed to participate in a fine arts career panel.

- Have students do research on other artists of their own choosing (for example, Mick Jagger, Tony Bennett, Rod Stewart, or Eric Clapton) who could be considered to be part of an "older group" in the popular music scene. Ask students to try to explain why these artists are still successfully recording and performing.

RESOURCES

Music Referenced in This Text

Alfred's Basic Piano Library, Levels 1–6, by Willard A. Palmer, Morton Manus, and Amanda Vick Lethco. Van Nuys, CA: Alfred Publishing Company, 1982–87.

Baroque Mix by Dawn Miller. San Diego: Neil A. Kjos Music Company, 1990.

Bastien Piano Basics, Levels 1–4, by Jane Bastien. San Diego: Neil A. Kjos Music Company, 1985.

"Blazing Trumpets" by Lynn Freeman Olson. Van Nuys, CA: Alfred Publishing Company, 1986.

Folk Songs for School and Camp by Jerry Silverman. Pacific, MO: Mel Bay Publications, 1991.

"Hero" by Walter Afanasieff and Mariah Carey. New York: Sony Music Publishing, 1993.

"Hornpipe" by John Jerrould. Cincinnati: Willis Music Company, 1985.

Jam Session by Ann Collins. Milwaukee: Hal Leonard Corporation, 1993.

Miniatures, Book 3, by Ruth Schonthal. Boston: Galaxy Music, 1964; distributed by ECS Publishing.

Mosaics, Book 1, ed. Marguerite Miller. Orem, UT: Sonos Music Resources, 1973.

Music and You, Grades 5–8. New York: Macmillan/McGraw-Hill, 1991.

The Music Connection, Grades 5–8. Parsippany, NJ: Silver Burdett Ginn, 1995.

Music Pathways by Lynn Freeman Olson, Louise Bianchi, and Marvin Blickenstaff. New York: Carl Fischer, 1983.

The Music Suite by Brian Moore and Robert Stephens. Grand Rapids, MI: Yamaha Corporation of America, 1995.

Ogilvy Keyboard Multiples, Book 1, by Jim and Susan Ogilvy. Denton, TX: Ogilvy Music, 1991.

One Plus One by Paul Sheftel. Van Nuys, CA: Alfred Publishing Company, 1986.

"Pianist on the Prowl" by Robert D. Vandall. Boulder, CO: Myklas Music Press, 1985.

Piano for the Developing Musician I, 3rd ed., by Martha Hilley and Lynn Freeman Olson. Minneapolis/St. Paul: West Publishing Company, 1993.

Pop! Goes the Piano, Book 1, by Lynn Freeman Olson. Van Nuys, CA: Alfred Publishing Company, 1985.

"Prelude: Song of the Harp" by C. Michael Ehrhardt. Cincinnati: Willis Music Company, 1984.

Share the Music, Grades 5–6. New York: Macmillan/McGraw-Hill, 1995.

"Two Flutes a-Fluting" by Edna Mae Burnam. Cincinnati: Willis Music Company, 1983.

World of Music, Grades 5–8. Parsippany, NJ: Silver Burdett Ginn, 1991.

Additional Resources

David Carr Glover Piano Library by David Carr Glover. Melville, NY: Belwin Mills, 1982; distributed by Warner Bros. Publications.

"Five Freaky Fugues" by Susan Mills Ulrich. Boston: Boston Music Company, 1994.

"Hanon in Rags" by Betty Guenther. Boston: Boston Music Company, 1994.

Maxwell Music Evaluation Notebooks by Carolyn Maxwell, including 1984 Update and Catch-Up, 1985 Update and Catch-Up, 1986 Update and Catch-Up, 1987–88 Update and Catch-Up, and 1989–90 Update and Catch-Up. Boulder, CO: Maxwell Music Evaluation, 1984–92.

Music in Education™: *A Technology Assisted Music Program* (four-volume curriculum) by Mitzi Kolar, Ernest Rideout, and Brian Moore. Grand Rapids, MI: Yamaha Corporation of America, 1995.

Music! Its Role and Importance in Our Lives by Charles Fowler. New York: Glencoe/McGraw-Hill, 1994.

PianoLab: An Introduction to Class Piano, 3rd ed., by Carolynn A. Lindeman. Belmont, CA: Wadsworth Publishing Company, 1996.

MENC Resources on Music and Arts Education Standards

Implementing the Arts Education Standards. Set of five brochures: "What School Boards Can Do," "What School Administrators Can Do," " What State Education Agencies Can Do," "What Parents Can Do," "What the Arts Community Can Do." 1994. #4022. Each brochure is also available in packs of 20.

Music for a Sound Education: A Tool Kit for Implementing the Standards. 1994. #1600.

National Standards for Arts Education: What Every Young American Should Know and Be Able to Do in the Arts. 1994. #1605.

Opportunity-to-Learn Standards for Music Instruction: Grades PreK–12. 1994. #1619.

Performance Standards for Music: Strategies and Benchmarks for Assessing Progress Toward the National Standards, Grades PreK–12. 1996. #1633.

Perspectives on Implementation: Arts Education Standards for America's Students. 1994. #1622.

"Prekindergarten Music Education Standards." Brochure. 1995. #4015 (set of 10).

The School Music Program—A New Vision: The K–12 National Standards, PreK Standards, and What They Mean to Music Educators. 1994. #1618.

Summary Statement: Education Reform, Standards, and the Arts. 1994. #4001 (pack of 10); #4001A (single copy).

"Teacher Education for the Arts Disciplines: Issues Raised by the National Standards for Arts Education." 1996. #1609.

Teaching Examples: Ideas for Music Educators. 1994. #1620.

The Vision for Arts Education in the 21st Century. 1994. #1617.

MENC's *Strategies for Teaching* Series

Strategies for Teaching Prekindergarten Music, compiled and edited by Wendy L. Sims. #1644.

Strategies for Teaching K–4 General Music, compiled and edited by Sandra L. Stauffer and Jennifer Davidson. #1645.

Strategies for Teaching Middle-Level General Music, compiled and edited by June M. Hinckley and Suzanne M. Shull. #1646.

Strategies for Teaching High School General Music, compiled and edited by Keith P. Thompson and Gloria J. Kiester. #1647.

Strategies for Teaching Elementary and Middle-Level Chorus, compiled and edited by Ann Roberts Small and Judy Bowers. #1648.

Strategies for Teaching High School Chorus, compiled and edited by Randal Swiggum. #1649.

Strategies for Teaching Strings and Orchestra, compiled and edited by Dorothy A. Straub, Louis Bergonzi, and Anne C. Witt. #1652.

Strategies for Teaching Middle-Level and High School Keyboard, compiled and edited by Martha F. Hilley and Tommie Pardue. #1655.

Strategies for Teaching Beginning and Intermediate Band, compiled and edited by Edward J. Kvet and Janet M. Tweed. #1650.

Strategies for Teaching High School Band, compiled and edited by Edward J. Kvet and John E. Williamson. #1651.

Strategies for Teaching Specialized Ensembles, compiled and edited by Robert A. Cutietta. #1653.

Strategies for Teaching Middle-Level and High School Guitar, compiled and edited by William E. Purse, James L. Jordan, and Nancy Marsters. #1654.

Strategies for Teaching: Guide for Music Methods Classes, compiled and edited by Louis O. Hall with Nancy R. Boone, George N. Heller, and Rosemary C. Watkins. #1656.

For more information on these and other MENC publications, write to or call MENC Publications Sales, 1806 Robert Fulton Drive, Reston, VA 20191-4348; 800-828-0229.